Blossom Tales

A Story of Menstrual Magic

Khamila Rose
Founder of ROSE GLOW CO

Copyright © 2025 by Khamila Rose

All rights reserved. No part of this publication may be reproduced, stored in a retrieval system, or transmitted in any form by any means, electronic, mechanical, photocopy, recording, or otherwise, without the prior permission of the publisher, except as provided by USA copyright law.

ISBN: 9798218714024

Contents

Foreword by Mike Rowe

The Garden

Uh Oh ...

The Nurse's Office

Blossoming

ROSE

All About Your Period

Period Products 101

Self-Care Spells

Healthy Habits

Track the Adventure

Menstrual Tracker

Daily Planner

Your Journey Continues

About the Author

Foreword

by Mike Rowe

I was filming an episode of *People You Should Know* at the Plumber's Union, Local 1, in Queens, when an eleven-year-old girl named Khamila Rose told me about the first time she got her period.

To be clear, I hadn't asked her for this information. I'd come to Union Local #1 that day to do a story on a foundation called Tools and Tiaras, a terrific organization that exposes young women to a variety of skilled trades. Khamila was there that day, along with dozens of other young girls to learn about careers in plumbing, and I was chatting her up as she was fitting two pipes together. At some point, I asked her what she did for fun, and Khamila told me she liked to write.

"Really?" I said. "What sort of things do you write about?"

"Well," she said, "I currently have two books published on Amazon."

"You're kidding," I said. "What are they called?"

"The first one is called *Sista Spy Squad*. It's the story of a young girl who discovers that her deceased parents used to be spies. Then she goes through a time portal, meets her new best friends, and follows in her parent's footsteps, as she and her team come face to face with The Sinister Six."

"I see," I said. "What about the second one?"

"The second one is called *Blossom Tales: A Story of Menstrual Magic*."

It was noisy in the workshop, and I thought she said, "Mental Magic." But no, she said, "Menstrual Magic," and Khamila took great pleasure in correcting me.

She repeated the title of her latest book nice and loud as the camera crew captured my reaction, which was pretty much what you'd expect from a grown man who suddenly finds himself having a conversation with a thirteen-year-old girl about a very different sort of plumbing.

Moments like that stick with you, and later that night, my curiosity got the better of me. I downloaded *Blossom Tales: A Story of Menstrual Magic* and read it on my computer. I thought it was great. A perfect story, really, for any young girl whose body was about to start behaving in a completely unfamiliar way. I thought it deserved to be out there in print, like a real book, so I called my mother's publisher, Jonathan Merkh, and told him about the thirteen-year-old aspiring female plumber who writes books about spy craft and menstruation. Jonathan read *Blossom Tales: A Story of Menstrual Magic* and quickly agreed to help get it published, if I agreed to write the foreword you're about to finish.

And that's how this book came to be.

Finally, I should tell you that I meet a lot of interesting people in my line of work, often by accident. Khamila Rose is one of those people, so it's fitting she wound up in an episode of *People You Should Know*, which you're welcome to watch on my YouTube Channel. Maybe she'll be a plumber when she grows up, or maybe she'll be a writer? Maybe she'll be neither or maybe she'll be both? All I know for sure is that right now, Khamila is a person you should know. A young girl, filled with more curiosity, more ambition, more work ethic, more imagination, and more entrepreneurial spirit that most adults. It's a privilege to help get her work to the masses, and I'm confident her words will bring a lot of comfort to thousands of young girls when they get their first visit from Aunt Flo.

Having said all that, turn the page, and let the blossoming begin . . .

THE GARDEN

"Bye, Willow! Have a great day at school!" my mom called out.

"Love you! I'll try!" I replied. "Or maybe not . . ." I mumbled to myself, because I didn't mreally love school.

I was on my way when I saw a local garden. *It's only 7:30, and school starts at 8:00 . . . so why not?* I thought to myself.

As I opened the gate, I noticed the vegetables and vines around me. Except, I wasn't here for that. I walked along the path that took me to my favorite part—the flowers. I twirled around and around until I got dizzy. I breathed in the fresh, delightful scent of the flowers.

I noticed how each and every one was beautiful and inspiring. They were all different, but they were all magical. I did a little cartwheel toward the pond that held the water lilies. I picked one up and dried it with its leaves. Then, I took out my phone and styled my hair, placing the magnificent flower on top, with guidance of my phone camera.

As I was about to shut off my phone, I caught a glimpse of the time. I thought I saw it wrong, but as I was about to check again, I heard the second school bell ring. I rushed out of the garden, making sure to close the gate on the way out.

I hope I make it in time! I thought to myself.

Imagine you are a flower in a garden. What kind of flower would you be and why?

_____
_____
_____
_____
_____
_____
_____
_____

What helps you grow strong and confident—like sunshine or rain helps a flower?

_____
_____
_____
_____
_____
_____
_____

UH OH...

And luckily, I made it past the school gates in time for the third and final bell. My classes went smoothly, and as soon as it was time for lunch, I wanted to race out of there. As I was about to get out of my seat, I felt a sticky, wet goo on the back of my pants.

I fully stood up to see what it was, but then I heard kids giggling. I checked my seat only to see . . . *Oh no! I have my PERIOD!*

I could feel my cheeks turning red from embarrassment as I heard the laughter in the classroom echoing the walls. I was calming myself down when someone said, "Ew! That's disgusting!" That only made everyone laughed harder. I cried running out of the classroom and didn't even bother getting my stuff from my desk.

"Oh, you should not be talking, Chad. Everyone knows you threw up in the hallway four times. Now that's disgusting! And since you might not be the brightest one here, I think you should shut your mouth and work on passing your test!"
I heard my bestie Harper say. And apparently, she followed me to the restroom.

Only a few seconds after I made it in the stall, she came running, calling my name, "Willow! Willow! Willow!"

"Yes?" I replied sniffing.

Harper opened the stall door. "Oh! Bestie, don't cry! Are you okay?"

"Yeah, I'm fine." I said, wiping my tears.
"Should we go to the nurse's office?" Harper asked.

"Yeah, I wanna know what to do!" I replied.

Pick one word that feels true for you today: magical, strong, ready, or supported. Why did you choose it?

_____
_____
_____
_____
_____
_____
_____
_____

Write about a time you felt proud of yourself, even if it was something small.

_____
_____
_____
_____
_____
_____
_____

THE NURSE'S OFFICE

"Hello, welcome to the nurse's office. May I please know who sent you?" the receptionist asked.

"Oh um, no one sent me. I decided to come here on my own. See, I have my period, and I want to know what to do about it," I explained.

"Ah, I understand. You can go visit Ms. Chilli right down the hall to your left."

"Thank you!" Harper and I said in unison.

And with that, the receptionist smiled from ear to ear and nodded her head.

As we opened the door, I was immediately attracted to the designs and posters on the wall.

I got startled by a voice behind me. "Hello! My name is Ms. Chilli. How can I help you?"

I turned around and said, "Hello! Um, so I kind of have my period, and I want to know what to do about it," I explained.

"Oh, I see. Don't worry; it's completely normal. Let's talk about what's happening. Do you have any questions or concerns?"

"I don't know what to do or expect," I said.

"That's perfectly okay. I'm here to help guide you through this blossoming into a new phase of your life. First, let's discuss the physical changes. Have you noticed any signs like breast development or hair growth?"

"Yes, I have," I said nervously.

"Great. That is a part of growing up. You might also experience changes in your body shape. It's all about becoming a young woman. Alongside these changes, you'll eventually have your first period."

"That's what happened in the restroom earlier."

"I understand. Your first period can be a surprise. It's a sign that your body is becoming capable of having children someday."

To manage it, you can use pads or tampons. Do you have any supplies with you?"

"No, I don't have anything."

"That's okay; we can help with that. I have some pads here in the office. You can use them for now. And remember, it's important to keep extra supplies in your bag for the future."

"Thanks. But, um, what exactly should I do with the pad?"

"Sure, I can explain. You'll need to peel off the backing of the pad and then place it in your underwear. Make sure it's centered and comfortable. Change it every few hours or when it feels full."

"How will I know when it's full?"

"You might start to feel wet or uncomfortable, so that's a good sign it's time for a change. And don't worry; you'll get the hang of it with practice."

"Okay. Is there anything else I should know?"

"Yes, it's important to keep good hygiene during your period. Make sure to wash your hands before and after changing your pad. Also, remember to wipe from front to back after using the toilet to prevent infection."

"Got it. Is there anything else I need to do?"

"Well, it's important to track your periods on a calendar. This way, you'll know when to expect your next one. And if you experience any severe cramps or heavy bleeding, please let a trusted adult know. It's important to take care of your health."

"Thanks for all the information. I was really worried at first, but I feel better now."

"I'm here to help, and I'm glad I could ease your worries. If you have any more questions in the future, don't hesitate to ask. You're on a wonderful journey of blossoming into a new woman, and I'm here to support you every step of the way."

"Thanks, Nurse. You're really nice."

"You're very welcome, sweetie. I'm always here to help you with any concerns you might have. Take care."

Which of these promises do you want to keep for yourself this month?

_____
_____
_____
_____
_____
_____
_____

Write your own promise that shows love and care for your growing body.

_____
_____
_____
_____
_____
_____
_____

Khamila says your body is like a flower blooming. What does that mean to you?

_____
_____
_____
_____
_____
_____
_____
_____

How does it feel to know you are part of a big circle of girls and women going through the same things?

_____
_____
_____
_____
_____
_____
_____
_____

BLOSSOMING

She was really nice, and I'm glad we could talk without it being weird or awkward. I was still a little nervous, but I was happy to get it off my chest. Two minutes after I stepped into the hallway, the bell rang and just like that school was done.

I was on my way home, and I decided to stop by the garden again. I went to where my favorite flowers were being held. I picked up a red rose, sat down, and thought about my day. I thought about all the crazy stuff happening, like me getting my period today. I felt upset, sad, and worried, but now I felt better.

I feel like I blossomed into a young lady.

I feel strong, powerful, and brave.

Think of a time something felt hard, but you got through it. What helped you?

___

If your period had a color or feeling, what would it be? Draw or describe it.

___

> "Like flowers blooming in a garden, every month is a petal of change on the way to becoming a beautiful young woman."
>
> Khamila Rose

ROSE GLOW CO.

How is your body feeling today—tired, energetic, calm, or sore?

___

What is one kind thing you can do for your body this week?

___

RADIANT

Embrace your inner glow with Rose Glow. Feel vibrant and beautiful throughout your period, exuding confidence in every step.

OPTIMISTIC

With Rose Glow, approach your period days with positivity. Stay hopeful and bright, knowing you have the support to tackle anything.

STRONG

Rose Glow empowers you to be resilient and powerful. Feel the strength within you, knowing you can handle anything that comes your way during your period.

EMPOWERED

Experience the empowerment that Rose Glow brings. Feel confident and in control, embracing your period as a natural part of who you are.

What did you notice about your body or mood today?

Is there anything about your cycle that surprised or interested you?

All About Your Period

What Is A Period?

It's a natural process where the body releases blood and tissue through the vagina. Menstruation typically lasts for a few days to a week and is a part of the menstrual cycle, which prepares the body for potential pregnancy.

How to Take Care of Your Period

Taking care of your period means using the right stuff for your body, eating good food 🍑, and drinking water 💧. Track your cycle to know when it's coming and get ready for it 🩸. Doing things that make you feel good 😊, moving around 🤸, and asking a grown-up if something feels weird are all important. Find things that make you comfy during your period so it doesn't feel yucky 🩸. Remember to take care of yourself when it happens! 🌸

Meet The MVP'S

Hey, friend! 🌟 Let's talk about the superheroes in your body: your ovaries, uterus, and hormones! 💁‍♀️🙆‍♀️ Imagine your ovaries as little egg pals—they hold eggs and make hormones to start the party. Then, your uterus is like a cozy home, all set for a baby if it decides to visit. And those hormones? They're like magical wizards inside you, making things happen, making you feel things, and making your period come along. Knowing about these cool things helps you understand your body's magic and be your own superhero! 💪✨

"

"Remember, you are your own cozy blanket on a chilly day. Wrap yourself in self-care and warmth."

Khamila Rose

ROSE GLOW CO.

Riding the Wave
Coping with Period Pains

Move Your Groove
Guess what? Moving your body can be like a superhero power against those cramps! Go for a light job, do some easy yoga poses, or even take a dip in the pool. It helps get your blood flowing and tells those cramps, "You're not the boss of me!"

Drink Up and Chow Down
Hydration is key, amigos! Sip on water like you're sipping on your favorite smoothie. Eating foods like fish, nuts, and leafy greens can be like a secret weapon against those cramps. And try avoiding too much of the salty, sugary stuff—it might make the cramps crankier!

Chill Vibes Only
Stress can make those cramps throw a bigger tantrum. Take deep breaths, try some relaxing yoga poses, or listen to your favorite tunes. It's like telling stress, "You can't hang with me today!"

Snuggle Time and Cozy Stuff
Make your space a comfy kingdom! Get your favorite blanket, wear those comfy PJs, and grab a bunch of pillows. Sometimes feeling cozy can make a big difference.

Write down three feelings you had this week. What made you feel that way?

_____
_____
_____
_____
_____
_____
_____

What helps you feel better when you're sad or frustrated?

_____
_____
_____
_____
_____
_____
_____

Period Products 101

Pads

- **Best organic pad:**
  Natracare Ultra Pads Super with Wings

- **Best pad for sports:**
  U by Kotex Fitness Ultra Thin Pads with Wings

- **Best pad for a heavy flow:**
  U by Kotex Security Feminine Maxi Pad with Wings

- **Best pad for sensitive skin:**
  Organyc Feminine Care Pads

- **Best pad for comfort:**
  Rael Organic Cotton Cover Pads

- **Best pad for a light flow:**
  Stayfree Ultra Thin Overnight Pads with Wings

- **Best overnight pad:**
  Always Extra Heavy Overnight Maxi Pads with Flexi-Wings

Tampons

- **Best tampons for sleep:**
  Tampax Pearl Overnight

- **Best tampons for sports:**
  Playtex Sport

- **Best tampons for a heavy flow:**
  Tampax Super-Plus

Period Underwear

- **Best period underwear for sleep:**
  Knix Super Leakproof

- **Best period underwear for sports:**
  SheThinx High-Waist

- **Best period underwear for a heavy flow:**
  Modibodi Maxi-24hrs

What changes have you noticed in your body lately?

_____
_____
_____
_____
_____
_____
_____

What is something you like about how your body is growing?

_____
_____
_____
_____
_____
_____
_____

Self Care Spells

Topics	Keypoints
Mindful Manifestation	Take moments throughout the day to pause and breathe. Inhale calmness, exhale stress. This simple act can transform the mundane into something magical.
Alchemy of Hydration	Water isn't just life's elixir; it's a self-care potion. Drink it abundantly to rejuvenate your body and spirit.
Nature's Enchantment	Step outside and soak in nature's beauty. Whether it's a walk in the woods or feeling the grass beneath your feet, nature's spell has an incredible power to life your spirits.
Journal Sorcery	Write down your thoughts, dreams, and aspirations. Pouring your heart onto paper can be a transformative act, freeing your mind and inviting positivity.
Dance of Joy	Lose yourself in the music and dance. Let the rhythm be your magic wand, casting away worries and inviting joy into your soul.

What helps you feel cozy or safe when you have your period?

_____
_____
_____
_____
_____
_____
_____

Make a "comfort list" with your favorite snacks, shows, songs, or activities for period days.

_____
_____
_____
_____
_____
_____
_____

HEALTHY HABITS
EXERCISE, NUTRITION, & SELF CARE

 ### 💧 **DRINK LOTS OF WATER:**

Water is super important! It helps with cramps and bloating, and it keeps you feeling good.

 ### 🍎 **EAT GOOD STUFF:**

Try to eat healthy foods like fruits, veggies, and stuff like whole grains and chicken. They can make you feel better during your period.

 ### 🏃‍♀️ **MOVE AROUND:**

You don't have to do hard exercise, but going for a walk or doing some easy yoga can help your cramps and make you feel happier.

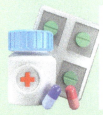

 ### 💊 **TAKE MEDICINE IF NEEDED:**

If your tummy hurts a lot, you can take medicine like your mom or dad says. Sometimes it helps!

HEALTHY HABITS
EXERCISE, NUTRITION, & SELF CARE

 ### 😴 *REST WHEN YOU FEEL TIRED:*
Your body might need more sleep during your period. It's totally okay to take naps or go to bed a bit earlier.

 ### 🧸 *DO RELAXING STUFF:*
Drawing, reading, or watching your favorite shows can help you relax and feel better.

 ### 👧♀️ *ASK FOR HELP:*
If you feel really bad or something seems weird, ask your mom, dad, or another grown-up you trust. They can help you feel better or take you to the doctor if needed.

 ### 👂 *LISTEN TO YOUR BODY:*
If something feels off or hurts a lot, it's important to tell someone you trust. Your body knows best!

Who is someone you trust to talk to about your period or feelings?

_____
_____
_____
_____
_____
_____
_____
_____

What would you say to help a friend who just got her first period?

_____
_____
_____
_____
_____
_____
_____
_____

What's one fun or kind thing you can do to celebrate your body this month?

___

If you've had your first period, what helped you feel okay? If not, what are you curious about?

___

TRACK THE ADVENTURE

Use a Calendar or App

Get a cool calendar or use an app on your phone. Write down when your period starts and stops each month.

Feelings and Body Changes

Jot down how you're feeling each day and any body changes like headaches, tummy aches, or feeling super energetic.

Remember Your Mood

Sometimes, you might feel extra happy or grumpy because of your cycle. Write down how you're feeling emotionally, like if you're really excited or a bit upset.

How Heavy Is Your Period?

💧 How Heavy Is Your Period?: Write if your period is light, medium, or heavy, and how many days it lasts.

Know About Ovulation

🌸 Whether you're thinking about having a baby or not, you might want to know when you're ovulating. You can use special kits or notice changes in your body like your temperature or the gooey stuff down there.

TRACK THE ADVENTURE

Think About Other Stuff

Things like what you eat, how much you move, and if you're feeling stressed can also affect your cycle. Write it down to see if there's a pattern.

Do It Regularly

Try to write this stuff down every month for a while. The more you write, the more you'll understand how your body works.

Talk to a Doctor

If something doesn't seem right, like if your period is too short or long, or you feel lots of pain, talk to a grown-up or a doctor.

MENSTURATION TRACKER

What's one healthy habit you want to practice during your period?
(Examples: drinking water, resting, stretching)

_____
_____
_____
_____
_____
_____
_____

What's something small you can do every day to take care of your body and mind?

_____
_____
_____
_____
_____
_____
_____

Sunday

TODAY'S SCHEDULE

Time	
6:00 AM	
7:00 AM	
8:00 AM	
9:00 AM	
10:00 AM	
11:00 AM	
12:00 PM	
1:00 PM	
2:00 PM	
3:00 PM	
4:00 PM	
5:00 PM	
6:00 PM	
7:00 PM	
8:00 PM	

NOTES :

GOALS :

TASKS

AFFIRMATION:

SONG OF THE DAY

Monday

TODAY'S SCHEDULE

Time	
6:00 AM	
7:00 AM	
8:00 AM	
9:00 AM	
10:00 AM	
11:00 AM	
12:00 PM	
1:00 PM	
2:00 PM	
3:00 PM	
4:00 PM	
5:00 PM	
6:00 PM	
7:00 PM	
8:00 PM	

NOTES:

GOALS:

TASKS

AFFIRMATION:

SONG OF THE DAY

Tuesday

TODAY'S SCHEDULE

Time	
6:00 AM	
7:00 AM	
8:00 AM	
9:00 AM	
10:00 AM	
11:00 AM	
12:00 PM	
1:00 PM	
2:00 PM	
3:00 PM	
4:00 PM	
5:00 PM	
6:00 PM	
7:00 PM	
8:00 PM	

NOTES :

GOALS :

TASKS

AFFIRMATION:

SONG OF THE DAY

Wednesday

TODAY'S SCHEDULE

Time	
6:00 AM	
7:00 AM	
8:00 AM	
9:00 AM	
10:00 AM	
11:00 AM	
12:00 PM	
1:00 PM	
2:00 PM	
3:00 PM	
4:00 PM	
5:00 PM	
6:00 PM	
7:00 PM	
8:00 PM	

NOTES :

GOALS :

TASKS

AFFIRMATION:

SONG OF THE DAY

Thursday

TODAY'S SCHEDULE

Time	
6:00 AM	
7:00 AM	
8:00 AM	
9:00 AM	
10:00 AM	
11:00 AM	
12:00 PM	
1:00 PM	
2:00 PM	
3:00 PM	
4:00 PM	
5:00 PM	
6:00 PM	
7:00 PM	
8:00 PM	

NOTES :

GOALS :

TASKS

AFFIRMATION:

SONG OF THE DAY

Friday

TODAY'S SCHEDULE

Time	
6:00 AM	
7:00 AM	
8:00 AM	
9:00 AM	
10:00 AM	
11:00 AM	
12:00 PM	
1:00 PM	
2:00 PM	
3:00 PM	
4:00 PM	
5:00 PM	
6:00 PM	
7:00 PM	
8:00 PM	

NOTES :

GOALS :

TASKS

AFFIRMATION:

SONG OF THE DAY

Saturday

TODAY'S SCHEDULE

Time	
6:00 AM	
7:00 AM	
8:00 AM	
9:00 AM	
10:00 AM	
11:00 AM	
12:00 PM	
1:00 PM	
2:00 PM	
3:00 PM	
4:00 PM	
5:00 PM	
6:00 PM	
7:00 PM	
8:00 PM	

NOTES :

GOALS :

TASKS

AFFIRMATION:

SONG OF THE DAY

Sunday

TODAY'S SCHEDULE

Time	
6:00 AM	
7:00 AM	
8:00 AM	
9:00 AM	
10:00 AM	
11:00 AM	
12:00 PM	
1:00 PM	
2:00 PM	
3:00 PM	
4:00 PM	
5:00 PM	
6:00 PM	
7:00 PM	
8:00 PM	

NOTES :

GOALS :

TASKS

AFFIRMATION:

SONG OF THE DAY

Monday

TODAY'S SCHEDULE

Time	
6:00 AM	
7:00 AM	
8:00 AM	
9:00 AM	
10:00 AM	
11:00 AM	
12:00 PM	
1:00 PM	
2:00 PM	
3:00 PM	
4:00 PM	
5:00 PM	
6:00 PM	
7:00 PM	
8:00 PM	

NOTES :

GOALS :

TASKS ♡♥♡

AFFIRMATION:

SONG OF THE DAY

Tuesday

TASKS

TODAY'S SCHEDULE

6:00 AM	
7:00 AM	
8:00 AM	
9:00 AM	
10:00 AM	
11:00 AM	
12:00 PM	
1:00 PM	
2:00 PM	
3:00 PM	
4:00 PM	
5:00 PM	
6:00 PM	
7:00 PM	
8:00 PM	

NOTES :

GOALS :

AFFIRMATION:

SONG OF THE DAY

Wednesday

TODAY'S SCHEDULE

Time	
6:00 AM	
7:00 AM	
8:00 AM	
9:00 AM	
10:00 AM	
11:00 AM	
12:00 PM	
1:00 PM	
2:00 PM	
3:00 PM	
4:00 PM	
5:00 PM	
6:00 PM	
7:00 PM	
8:00 PM	

NOTES :

GOALS :

TASKS

AFFIRMATION:

SONG OF THE DAY

Thursday

TODAY'S SCHEDULE

6:00 AM	
7:00 AM	
8:00 AM	
9:00 AM	
10:00 AM	
11:00 AM	
12:00 PM	
1:00 PM	
2:00 PM	
3:00 PM	
4:00 PM	
5:00 PM	
6:00 PM	
7:00 PM	
8:00 PM	

NOTES :

GOALS :

TASKS

AFFIRMATION:

SONG OF THE DAY

Friday

TODAY'S SCHEDULE

Time	
6:00 AM	
7:00 AM	
8:00 AM	
9:00 AM	
10:00 AM	
11:00 AM	
12:00 PM	
1:00 PM	
2:00 PM	
3:00 PM	
4:00 PM	
5:00 PM	
6:00 PM	
7:00 PM	
8:00 PM	

NOTES :

GOALS :

TASKS

_____
_____
_____
_____
_____

AFFIRMATION:

SONG OF THE DAY

Saturday

TODAY'S SCHEDULE

Time	
6:00 AM	
7:00 AM	
8:00 AM	
9:00 AM	
10:00 AM	
11:00 AM	
12:00 PM	
1:00 PM	
2:00 PM	
3:00 PM	
4:00 PM	
5:00 PM	
6:00 PM	
7:00 PM	
8:00 PM	

NOTES :

GOALS :

TASKS

AFFIRMATION:

SONG OF THE DAY

Sunday

TODAY'S SCHEDULE

Time	
6:00 AM	
7:00 AM	
8:00 AM	
9:00 AM	
10:00 AM	
11:00 AM	
12:00 PM	
1:00 PM	
2:00 PM	
3:00 PM	
4:00 PM	
5:00 PM	
6:00 PM	
7:00 PM	
8:00 PM	

NOTES :

GOALS :

TASKS

AFFIRMATION:

SONG OF THE DAY

Monday

TODAY'S SCHEDULE

Time	
6:00 AM	
7:00 AM	
8:00 AM	
9:00 AM	
10:00 AM	
11:00 AM	
12:00 PM	
1:00 PM	
2:00 PM	
3:00 PM	
4:00 PM	
5:00 PM	
6:00 PM	
7:00 PM	
8:00 PM	

NOTES :

GOALS :

TASKS

AFFIRMATION:

SONG OF THE DAY

Tuesday

TODAY'S SCHEDULE

Time	
6:00 AM	
7:00 AM	
8:00 AM	
9:00 AM	
10:00 AM	
11:00 AM	
12:00 PM	
1:00 PM	
2:00 PM	
3:00 PM	
4:00 PM	
5:00 PM	
6:00 PM	
7:00 PM	
8:00 PM	

NOTES :

GOALS :

TASKS

AFFIRMATION:

SONG OF THE DAY

Wednesday

TODAY'S SCHEDULE

Time	
6:00 AM	
7:00 AM	
8:00 AM	
9:00 AM	
10:00 AM	
11:00 AM	
12:00 PM	
1:00 PM	
2:00 PM	
3:00 PM	
4:00 PM	
5:00 PM	
6:00 PM	
7:00 PM	
8:00 PM	

NOTES :

GOALS :

TASKS

AFFIRMATION:

SONG OF THE DAY

Thursday

TODAY'S SCHEDULE

Time	
6:00 AM	
7:00 AM	
8:00 AM	
9:00 AM	
10:00 AM	
11:00 AM	
12:00 PM	
1:00 PM	
2:00 PM	
3:00 PM	
4:00 PM	
5:00 PM	
6:00 PM	
7:00 PM	
8:00 PM	

NOTES :

GOALS :

TASKS

AFFIRMATION:

SONG OF THE DAY

Friday

TODAY'S SCHEDULE

Time	
6:00 AM	
7:00 AM	
8:00 AM	
9:00 AM	
10:00 AM	
11:00 AM	
12:00 PM	
1:00 PM	
2:00 PM	
3:00 PM	
4:00 PM	
5:00 PM	
6:00 PM	
7:00 PM	
8:00 PM	

NOTES :

GOALS :

TASKS

_____
_____
_____
_____
_____

AFFIRMATION:

SONG OF THE DAY

Saturday

TODAY'S SCHEDULE

Time	
6:00 AM	
7:00 AM	
8:00 AM	
9:00 AM	
10:00 AM	
11:00 AM	
12:00 PM	
1:00 PM	
2:00 PM	
3:00 PM	
4:00 PM	
5:00 PM	
6:00 PM	
7:00 PM	
8:00 PM	

NOTES :

GOALS :

TASKS

AFFIRMATION:

SONG OF THE DAY

Sunday

TODAY'S SCHEDULE

Time	
6:00 AM	
7:00 AM	
8:00 AM	
9:00 AM	
10:00 AM	
11:00 AM	
12:00 PM	
1:00 PM	
2:00 PM	
3:00 PM	
4:00 PM	
5:00 PM	
6:00 PM	
7:00 PM	
8:00 PM	

NOTES :

GOALS :

TASKS

AFFIRMATION:

SONG OF THE DAY

Monday

TODAY'S SCHEDULE

Time	
6:00 AM	
7:00 AM	
8:00 AM	
9:00 AM	
10:00 AM	
11:00 AM	
12:00 PM	
1:00 PM	
2:00 PM	
3:00 PM	
4:00 PM	
5:00 PM	
6:00 PM	
7:00 PM	
8:00 PM	

NOTES :

GOALS :

TASKS

AFFIRMATION:

SONG OF THE DAY

Tuesday

TODAY'S SCHEDULE

Time	
6:00 AM	
7:00 AM	
8:00 AM	
9:00 AM	
10:00 AM	
11:00 AM	
12:00 PM	
1:00 PM	
2:00 PM	
3:00 PM	
4:00 PM	
5:00 PM	
6:00 PM	
7:00 PM	
8:00 PM	

NOTES :

GOALS :

TASKS

AFFIRMATION:

SONG OF THE DAY

Wednesday

TODAY'S SCHEDULE

Time	
6:00 AM	
7:00 AM	
8:00 AM	
9:00 AM	
10:00 AM	
11:00 AM	
12:00 PM	
1:00 PM	
2:00 PM	
3:00 PM	
4:00 PM	
5:00 PM	
6:00 PM	
7:00 PM	
8:00 PM	

NOTES :

GOALS :

TASKS

AFFIRMATION:

SONG OF THE DAY

Thursday

TODAY'S SCHEDULE

Time	
6:00 AM	
7:00 AM	
8:00 AM	
9:00 AM	
10:00 AM	
11:00 AM	
12:00 PM	
1:00 PM	
2:00 PM	
3:00 PM	
4:00 PM	
5:00 PM	
6:00 PM	
7:00 PM	
8:00 PM	

NOTES :

GOALS :

TASKS

AFFIRMATION:

SONG OF THE DAY

Friday

TODAY'S SCHEDULE

6:00 AM	
7:00 AM	
8:00 AM	
9:00 AM	
10:00 AM	
11:00 AM	
12:00 PM	
1:00 PM	
2:00 PM	
3:00 PM	
4:00 PM	
5:00 PM	
6:00 PM	
7:00 PM	
8:00 PM	

NOTES :

GOALS :

TASKS

_____

_____

_____

_____

_____

AFFIRMATION:

SONG OF THE DAY

Saturday

TODAY'S SCHEDULE

6:00 AM	
7:00 AM	
8:00 AM	
9:00 AM	
10:00 AM	
11:00 AM	
12:00 PM	
1:00 PM	
2:00 PM	
3:00 PM	
4:00 PM	
5:00 PM	
6:00 PM	
7:00 PM	
8:00 PM	

NOTES :

GOALS :

TASKS

AFFIRMATION:

SONG OF THE DAY

Sunday

TODAY'S SCHEDULE

Time	
6:00 AM	
7:00 AM	
8:00 AM	
9:00 AM	
10:00 AM	
11:00 AM	
12:00 PM	
1:00 PM	
2:00 PM	
3:00 PM	
4:00 PM	
5:00 PM	
6:00 PM	
7:00 PM	
8:00 PM	

NOTES :

GOALS :

TASKS

AFFIRMATION:

SONG OF THE DAY

Monday

TODAY'S SCHEDULE

Time	
6:00 AM	
7:00 AM	
8:00 AM	
9:00 AM	
10:00 AM	
11:00 AM	
12:00 PM	
1:00 PM	
2:00 PM	
3:00 PM	
4:00 PM	
5:00 PM	
6:00 PM	
7:00 PM	
8:00 PM	

TASKS

NOTES :

GOALS :

AFFIRMATION:

SONG OF THE DAY

Your Journey Continues

Dear Bloomer,

Congratulations on taking this important step in your blossoming journey! Just like Willow in our story, you're blossoming into an amazing young girl with strength and magic all your own.

Always remember, your period is just one part of the beautiful transformation unfolding in your body. It might feel unfamiliar, frightening, or even overwhelming at times, but you are never alone. Every girl with a period goes through similar experiences, and each journey is unique and special.

Always Remember

- You are magical – Your body is doing exactly what it's supposed to do.
- You are strong – Even on days when cramps or emotions feel intense and unbearable.
- You are prepared – With knowledge and supplies to handle whatever comes your way.
- You are supported – By friends, family, and your Rose Glow community.

Your Period Promises

I promise to...

- Be kind to my body and listen when it needs rest.
- Celebrate this natural part of growing up.
- Ask questions when I'm confused or concerned.
- Share my knowledge to help others when they need it.
- Remember I am beautiful, powerful, and worthy every day of the month.

A Note from Khamila

"Your period journey is as unique as a fingerprint, as natural as flowers blooming in spring. Some days it will be sunshine; others might bring rain clouds. But remember, after every rainfall, flowers grow even stronger. You're not just experiencing a period; you're embracing your power, connecting with generations of girls and women before you who have flowed and blossomed with this same rhythm of life.

Whenever you feel uncertain, remember that you are part of something magical and meaningful. Like the cycles of the moon that light up our darkest nights, your body has its own beautiful wisdom.

May you embrace your own unique journey with courage and grace. Always remember the strength that blooms within you, is a natural and powerful force. Nurture yourself, allow yourself to blossom, and face every new chapter with the unwavering spirit of a true blossom tale.

Bloom proudly,

Khamila Rose

"Every month is a chance to bloom again, stronger and more beautiful than before."

Journal

Thank you for reading Blossom Tales: A Story of Menstrual Magic!

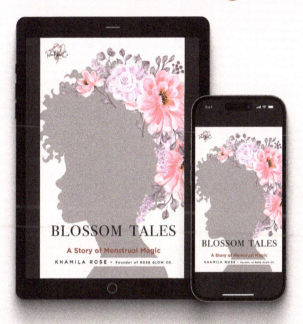

Use the QR Code to download a Free Ebook version.

www.ingramcontent.com/pod-product-compliance
Lightning Source LLC
LaVergne TN
LVHW071412110725
815935LV00019B/421

Blossom Tales: A Story of Menstrual Magic follows a young girl on her daily walk past a local garden. Today is special – she just got her first period! Join her magical journey filled with surprises, friendship, and self-discovery. The garden becomes a place of whispers and wisdom. Through ups and downs, she learns the magic of embracing changes and self-acceptance. This heartwarming tale celebrates courage, friendship, and the enchanting power of growing up. Get ready for a magical journey through the garden of life!

KHAMILA ROSE
FOUNDER OF ROSEGLOW

Meet Khamila Rose, the cookie queen from Brooklyn! She not only bakes tasty custom shortbread cookies but also runs a period kit business. Khamila is on a mission to make every girl feel confident and comfortable during that time of the month. With her thoughtful and stylish kits, she's turning periods into moments of strength and self-expression.

ISBN 979-8-218-71402-4

IG: @KHAMILAROSE